Uncommon Place

ALSO BY GERRIE FELLOWS

Technologies and Other Poems (Polygon, 1990)
The Powerlines (Polygon, 2000)
The Duntroon Toponymy (Mariscat, 2001)
Window for a Small Blue Child (Carcanet, 2007)
The Body in Space (Shearsman Books, 2014)

Gerrie Fellows

Uncommon Place

Shearsman Books

First published in the United Kingdom in 2019 by
Shearsman Books
50 Westons Hill Drive
Emersons Green
BRISTOL
BS16 7DF

Shearsman Books Ltd Registered Office
30–31 St. James Place, Mangotsfield, Bristol BS16 9JB
(this address not for correspondence)

www.shearsman.com

ISBN 978-1-84861-635-6

Contents

Uncommon Place

Transitional
(Loch Ossian to the Water of Nevis)

i

Under the wind turbine
birch wood   tattered bunting
pegs & stacked coal
spots of colour
vanish into thick air

Elevations levelled by cloud
islands in mist   a revelation
divulged by the flight of birds
                white-bellied   over water
                             huzzas of shooting parties
                             rowed from the pierhead
                             this place once was
where I begin from

        under the stilled blades
        a multitude of voices
        raised at departure
        the harp   played by the wind

ii

Into a nowhere
bound by tracks   old tracings
yet hard underfoot
                             the iron route of the railway
                             held by brushwood and earth
                             (new trunks for old in buried peat)
                             follows the herding and herded ghosts

Over springy selvedge
mind floats   wisps of bog cotton

      Above the loch
      the train   secret but for sound
      in its belt of leaves

                iii

What is a place:
a titled lodge
under a leek-green crag
on a loch whose name meant   *to cease*
while houses yet stood at its head

                a halt on the drove roads
                a market at Kinlochtreig
                for drovers and thieves
                    vanished

before the shores were inundated
waters raised
to power the Alcan smelter

or drained   to a trace landscape
of meanders   contours
of fine gravel   water-rippled
as the ripple marks in the rock
the continuous transformation
of sand to rock   of rock to sand
of water to power through distant pipes

iv

Ahead   low cloud in the gap
mountains named and renamed
                    a speculation

the river
a link around which perspective swings
summits   clouds and blueing air
all   in our binocular vision

Names succeed one another
from east to west   yet place is flowing
                         as the river is
                         as a path is
through bell heather and cross-leaved heath
                    as walking seems to be

                        the successive steps
of our gait beside the Abhainn Rath
past alder and bog myrtle   moving
upwards against its rushing down

                    voices in a solitude
in the strings of the wind   the river's music
peregrine's solitary mew   dragonflies
a coupled zither
          tumble rings of gold through air

water
tumbling over schist and porphyry
a sculpture of folded upheavals   turbulent
as weather across the quartzite summits   flows
over the jumbled successions of geology

makes a truth of our not knowing

v

Evening at Meanach
billies, rock-balanced
my windblown flame
makes slow tea

                                    Peopled once   a habitation
is a place a gable end
a fire in the hearth   at the bothy, at skeletal Luibeilt

Before the shepherds   the transitory smoke of thieves
                                    making meals of bannock
                                    and cattle blood
                                    herding stolen beasts

after them   transient
we unfold our rolled alloys, best titanium
make a high summer habitat
under flysheets and netted inners
                populous again

            Over transitory kitchens
            at dusk   a smoke of midges

                        vi

                    Each step a questioning
            of balance over water   verve of crossing
from stone to stone
                over the shoaling river
    our good fortune in a dry summer yet deep in air
                        waist deep the echo of a torrent

To the watershed
               a narrative of crossings
             the wanderings of a river feint
of our faint path
but who needs it now
when we can dance over dried-out peat
with only clegs to prickle us

                deep in rain or snow melt
                the meadows   impassable bog
                the river   unfordable
                the watershed unreachable
                              an impasse

              this point in space
from which on a summer's day
to frame a viewpoint   in deep
                          among folds of tilted earth
                          where air was rock

the summits
tethered at last to their names   never stop shifting
play us for fools and strangers

Is place passed through   or does it pass through us

quartz grain, bedrock, microbial soil

                place   changing its nature

Span (1)

In the birch leaves
lightness moves
fire quick

inhabits waste spaces
makes new
the burnt ground

brittle whips
the wind snaps

lives like humans

Seeded

(Dawyck Botanic Gardens, mid-September)

A chill
among uncut grasses

of an almost wild place
quick birds in the undergrowth   Betula ermanii
papery barked   flares gold

almost wild
as if in an orchard gone to seed
                      small dark berries of Prunus grayana
feathery grasses   creeping buttercup   Miyama Cherry
seedheads of sorrel

almost wild
(as is said of a garden
run wild in a season's brief generation)
yet tended:

                a garden of the found   collected, transported
                                               as seed or cutting:

                cinnamon-barked   Rhododendron calophytum
                                         carried from Sichuan
                                         (by 'Chinese' Wilson)

                felt leaves of   Rhododendron bureavii
                                 borne from Yunnan
to this damp island
where folded lichens grow
                on patchy barked   Nippon Maple
                                    (native to the mountains
                                    of southern Japan)

Under my hand: peeling Flaky Bark fir
                                (a slow motion in thin air)

corky bark of Sequoiadendron giganteum
                                (resistant to the fires of its native place
                                seeds falling from scorched cones
                                regenerate on ash)

In labels rubbed for knowledge   place is elsewhere
                                (an echo
                                a suggestion of the exotic)

                                Korean whitebeam
                                Spirea japonica

           grow in this shady glen
        in starred and creeping mosses
        native to this place
                                the Nikko fir's purple cones
flared and empty   flung outward
seeding in this new ground:

this place
to which after 8,000 years   Pinus sylvestris
                                has become native

          earth enmeshed by roots of birch   oak
                             Fagus sylvatica

           invisible entanglements   Cep, False Chanterelle
              fleetingly revealed
                           beechmast
          lifting on a swirl of wind

Air and water enter it: leaves turn light to sap

                           (vision to substance)

molecules of water

            restlessly travelling

transformative   of tree, soil, rock   of place

                  flow through this particular habitat

                      this particular climate

                      of temperate cold

transformed

        through tree, soil, rock   becoming place

Span (2)

Radiant cells   thin-walled
to carry sap through spring wood

porous, diffusing nets
fixed in circumferences of dark and light

our blood's quick molecules
a restless encompassing

the trees' slow circulation
of time and weather

Margin Note
(Glen Fruin)

i
rusted wire
fence posts silvered, lichenous
make the margin

odd human
working my way uphill
against water   against
time marked by intervals
or flowing   as water
        undivided
over steep, damp banks
of sedge and primrose
cantilevered rowan

the fence turned
encloses   (if not animals)
a shape and space

tussock and sphagnum

the ground we walk up into
invisible   yet divisible
        an owned object

        the unfenced open

ii
on the wind   voices
blown against us
the plaint of sheep
without sign
of a skittering flock

a sheep dog call
the high, invisible larks

each indivisible note

iii
DANGER
MILITARY FIRING RANGE
No Entry signs
one after another on the ridge
NO ACCESS
WHEN RED FLAGS
OR LIGHTS
ARE DISPLAYED
one faded, another new

a kind of fence
between wind drift   pale mat grass

perforated by place

Watershed
(Glen Affric to Loch Duich)

i
Intent on our destination
hard core under boot soles
the track a drum
fenced from lightness
of birch leaves, sinuous pine
fenced from water
under hill names scooped with snow

bird calls cross the wire
we walk between
high strung instrument
the flickering wren has no part of
nor the pine marten
doling dark scats in indented dust

racing spokes overtake us
at our walking pace
come down at last to the loch
find ourselves   without access
to what was once grazing
zoned from human intervention
by human intent

ii
zoned from grazing deer
fenced saplings   and pines
older than we can imagine
in our embodied counting
(at the pace of racers   simple walkers
in our one-time lifetime)

grandmother pine
going under   in slow motion

home to insect and lichen
nutrient to nutrient soil
how strange to us

serpentine,   cracked beauty

iii
as if we could live otherwise
in our ever-moving at evening
deeper   into the moine
against the flow
of the long east-flowing river
against ice
against the scour of glacial trough
into the catchment

the rocks of the moine slide us
over buried levels
(now we're in deep time   and counting)
hitch us also a little sinister, infinitesimally
                shift
the precipitous breached ridges

iv
        flit past the pace of geology
or ice   thinking them stilled
            to where even a river

in a space of grass and moss
is an almost imperceptible welling

before moment
            to momentum
                        /falling
                            headlong

                    we are
held
in gravity's tip
over the slowest transformations
of rock   over/
metasediments, unimaginable
over
        into
                    into

Footnote

light-footed
footering off the path

jolted loose

how heavy-footed also
downbeat thumper of tubs

monomaniac drummer
of struck sounds

without echo
the flat dumb beat

leaden   as of colour
muffled   as of cloud

a plumb weight
in the temperate zone's

shifting light

yet footloose
absurdly happy

Border (1)
(Windy Gyle to the Cheviot)

We walk a line in air   a fence
run through cloudberry and ling
as once by broad sword in lorded-over lands
broad swathe towards ocean
where the border swithers   held by a river

silvered fence post   wire silvered
bog cotton and heather

wind across the fells' low-lying blue
blows over rough ground
undiversified   the uses of the marginal
a riot of seedheads   bright moss

flagged orange of the bumble bee
hill-topping in blaeberry and sphagnum
skylark over cairn-studded bog
seems to sing of sky and rising ground
     signals mate and territory

On the common border
our fellow walkers guessed at by voice
as we'd be guessed at   turning north
(home   though we were not born to it
our voices not of it)

cloud over the summit blinds us
binds us to the littoral
high granite declines to sediment
unconformity   haar-lapped coast

we walk a tensile edge on this high rig
where place names are of hope
air between the wires nets us   lets us breathe

weather and history shift in us
ideas of country more nebulous
than place   in which we meet
lifting north-westward   cloud-scudded
ground   we go skylarking over

Border (2)

In cloud to a plinth in a quagmire
(creeping buttercup burns in mist)

the slabbed summit path
an airdropped weight

it would have taken an army
in sight of Trimontium to set

new marchers over old marches
on reused mill flags flecked with rust

once hectic with hoists   and pitched
at angles to their deposition

as sand grains   particles of mud adrift
half a world away in salt water or fresh

silted down to rippled bands   embedded
rock transposed before quarry or manufactory

eroding now along the border's transient fix

above sphagnum cotton-grass crowberry
decomposing to imperfect carbon

over the earth's tectonic shifts

Catchment
(Tweed's Well to Hart Fell)

Flung outwards   feathering into air
stalked green and purple waves
bees in a scramble of iron red clover
to walk the watershed

a fancy   to name beginnings
a welling, a sandstone plinth
to count water miles and altitudes
Powskein Burn to Crown of Scotland
Whitehope Burn to Whitehope Knowe
Annanhead to Solway

       a network   no single source
       each mossy trickle   a thread
       of movement   like a trace
       on a map of the blood

or a trick of two dimensions
false as the network of a family tree
conjured towards a bloodhead

       in three dimensions
       pulsed outward to lungs, to fingertips
       the fronded capillaries
       lose themselves in fractals
       blood seeps   intricate welling
       drawn back   recirculates

From the watershed
the shed water   an issue of names
mapped
to boundary river or dividing estuary

a preamble
through ground permeable as skin
mineral salts suspended
        towards ocean
        in turbulent velocities

to rise   out of the map's two dimensions
into another order   dispersed

      nameless   the droplets fall over us
      are felt in our fingertips

minute codes   pulsing under our skin
the nervous system with its filigrees
its tendrils
        catching
            catching

       an echo in ourselves

Blank under cloud barytes
(Muirshiel to Misty Law)

Into the weather
on cracked basaltic lavas, sheeny between tussocks

under white - grey - blue
high pylons crossing
and the spring birds   only sounds
in the sounds of last night's rain   rills
streaming off the Muirshiel to the rift of the Clyde

The sky we are under   busy with cloud and colour
clumped with light
the wind enters
slams shut its gunmetal stratus   over jolted footsteps
                                    the ruts of wheels and hooves
until all that is luminous
is a last glowing rail of northern light

Into the leaden, blank under cloud
                        walking the footfall of miners
        between iron track and sky   the settling ponds'
                            unreflective puddles of smoky rain

What's left
fenced with wire
in the deep cut of the mine   barytes' glittering fragments
                                 of cracked pink   a history
                                 of the men who worked it
in the undercut rim of the burn   in the gullies   in the twist
                                 of invisible seams

What's luminous here

    denser than water
    deeper than shafts
    sunk into flickering snow

white jigsaw on flattened grass

    tipped and broken bodies
    rock and metal crushed

What shines
is sleet blown in our faces   pearly luminescence

then nothing but dancing
over bogs
over jewelled green hollows   a cosmetic radiance
    in the pattern and patina of porcelain
    paint and paper   white pigment
    denser than mist

closes law and muir
to fence line   trig point   cairn
to just ourselves   half-seen
in a backing wind
in the cyclone's deep low   the echo
    of men, half-heard   underground
    of women in the ruined houses
    in the crushing mill
in the roar of a waterfall   children   clatter of ponies

The high aircraft crossing   sounds invisible to us
sunlit   over flat and curving earth

What's luminous here   shines as barytes shines
    blank under cloud

smoke screen   fragments
(Ayrshire to Galloway)

Tarfessock   (697m)
from sunlight under upturned layers
through vapour   afoot in grass

turned up   underfoot
a canister shucked from a rucksack
its shining pin, unloosed   a smoke screen
      call it grenade, hand
      (call it L83A2)

split branches, loosed   (agency, human)
in this treeless   (call it) training ground
bivouac detritus ditched by squaddies
erratic   between granite boulders
      ice-carried towards us

      call it brae or rig
      (call it NX413 888)

a tumbled wall
above the map's last contour
clouded-in   780m on Kirriereoch
      call it lost   (spot height 786m
      a pinpoint in a smoke screen)

the descent, a bearing   unsighted
a broken wall   fence posts (e)merging
each next (NX414 870)   obliterated
where iron disintegrates in pooled lead shot

to blocks of forest   a river crossing
(NX388 877)   safe over   (call it safe
thigh deep in pooling dark)

to take high tea on the high track
(black with seeded rolls)   (NX388 881)
rain splintering   quartered
by our headtorch beams   (call it black
seeded with light   as if through driven snow)

to find the road (un-numbered)   cloudbound
each next diamond to diamond sign
a lit flare in full beam

Fire-working
(Galloway: Woodhead Mine to Cairnsgarroch)

Before the night's bright works
(Fawkes' flame of a name gone into fable)
from Green Well to Garryhorn
fenced in a fire of leaves

> *where Lag, the King's man,*
> *pursued a people gathered to worship*
> the lead mine's standing debris
> shadows forth men *raising stones*
> *the vein   ore-bearing, trending north-east*

all that's visible   ruined smelt mill crushing mill
stone-capped flues running upslope
half-tumbled chimneys void of fumes

bracken as if in flame   autumn grass
heralds bonfires circling sparks   flicker
of bodies moving in the flare of furnaces

ores brought dull out of the earth
        (18oz of silver in one ton of lead)

> *The washing and scumming done by boys*
> *in all weathers*
> *but for the absolute freezing of water*

shaft hollows, subsidence cones

> top, middle and deep adit
> 11 fathom level   25 fathom level
> *a series of wet, dirty, almost perpendicular ladders*

the encircled nature of the place
a triangular warning   rock cut   echo

of shawled women   a scattering tide
of scrubbed children
men released into daylight grasses   bird song
the word of the Lord in Lamloch kirk
given way to *sheepfold, ruinous*

densities of conifer we turn away from
knock our boots over Knockower
owerlooking the high sunlit stalks o turbines
stalks of grasses   bleached seedheads
                    a windblown scatter

> *from galleries damp and ill-ventilated,*
> *loaded with fumes of gunpowder*
> *stone's shattered particles*

From the northernmost rig of the Rhinns
invisible the plain we drove by   the route
of coal and lime   ingots traded outward
the malleable material of piped water
roofwork of cathedrals
            (the high-vaulted word of the Lord)

our ring of walking makes a bow around the lead mine
yellow as whin   a wreath for the dead

> *lost to a false or incautious step*
> *to the explosion of their blasting charges*
> *to chronic afflictions of the chest*

but the map's markers stand for fabled solitaries
John Dempster martyred by Lag's dragoons
boulders for a king   *Bruce's Stone Bruce's Well*
stopping places as fugitive as the man himself
the myths of place   set down
among lumpen facts of glacial moraine

evident to the eye
only the tussocks' burnt umber   ATV tracks on shaly ground

the township's half visible standings   half-
submerged mounds of fieldbanks
runrig that merges into grazing

a schoolhouse wall blank of scribbled names
a gable end   a vanished row
named once in the common parlance of families

> *here lived Marion Moffat or Bone*
> *here lived John Paterson   Margaret Paterson*
> *here lived Thomas Hope   Isabell Gracie*

Across the worked-out ores
shafts and levels dark under us
air dims to haze   a translucence tinged with rose

as if the lead mine's fire were stored there
lighting the night with the spark of their names

> *Thomas Weir, Lead Miner*
> *Elizabeth Tennant, Widow*
> *John MacMath, Lead Miner's Labourer*
> *Sophia Harvey, Needlewoman*
> *John Russel, Lead washer*
> *Agnes MacPherson, Scholar*
> *David Moffat, Lead Miner*
> *Mary McKendrick, Lead Miner's Wife*

Timeline with Found Objects
(Three poems from Harrapool, Skye)

i

First or last   conical stacks built upwards
slabs lifted dried turned dried
spring to summer repeated

white peat a flare to fire
half-rotted down to earth
a ground of discoloured stainings

not sienna nor umber
the tonal earths of other places
moisture-laden colour of peat

the blade cuts down through
leaves and roots   float of sphagnum
interred   anoxic

stacked time
of the peat column's seamless levels
to the treeline

reveals
what it is we were making of this earth
climate   tillage   cut back to a spark

volcanic ash   residues of pollen
the long burn of blue peat

down to clay   glaciated rock
what is found there

        an acorn's half cup   stained dark
        knotted bog oak bark
        sheen of a twig

debris of the treeline
fallen back in time
forward into our hands

ii

The croft house
a space we occupy
between so many others   arriving
week by week   year on year
to eat   sleep   be   here and now
                              and then
(our comings and goings
already in our own past)

we are observers of doorframes
windows on a time   (even our own uncertain)
through the longitudinal data of history
back to long strip cultivation
a map survey, 1876
the croft house here, we think
and its ruined original

but the map offers
no knowledge of who it is we look for
as if we could find them in roof space rafters
the shape of a window   (the shape
of mouths and of the language forming)
the unverified evidence of our own observation

the language in which we speak of this
a structure both solid and open   known and uncertain

        but there in its place
        framed   a small view of
        a mountain   unchanged

in the scale of vision
shifts ceaselessly
in cloud and sunlight

iii

Why count uncounted shells
or fossil shells   or the simpler tally
of beachcombers searching the fossil line
between them time   figured in weeks or years

what is carried away   what remains
in the soft matrix of siltstone or mudstone
hard enough   each in its hard niche

the tidal wash uncovers the friable layers
a time exposure   like a camera
(a memory   our fossil photographs)
or the human eye   blinking open

the movement in this is a shell
without propulsion in a drift of silt   without
its soft-bodied creature   its tenacious inhabitant
it is only a house   a husk
laid down and overlaid

a movement of waves against mud
the push of deep ocean's chargeless turbines
sifting grains   physical and minute

    compacted beds of fossil oysters
    devil's toenails plunged into mud
    fanned bivalves   scalloplike
    prized black spirals and their cupped negatives

a lightness or weight
carried home
to windowsill or boundary wall

my hand lifts and places

Between Geology and Air
(Question and answer after Ingrid Calame)

How can we live
as if in a child's painting:
    earth sky
what is human between them

how can we live
between sky and earth
and not be compressed

the air in the alveoli
    dense as if water
were flowing through us

Under our footsteps:
    graffiti bones
    the fossil layers
    the mineral chains

attach us by lightsome metals
    mined to make
    our miracles

    Earth pushes up
through our footsoles
    air spins us
in its thinning spheres
    time flies through us

Rope Piece
(The fact of form after Bill Bollinger)

Were they intended   these taut solids
as a steep-angled valley
                                        made of air
the mind plays rope tricks with

the material   shifting perspective
less solid than woodblock
a Chinese ink landscape   of disappearance

illusion   or a walking into
(as happens in that other
enclosed   enfolded)   space
                                        plays with me
opens   what I enter

Let's not call it landscape (that framed
                viewpoint)
nor land   which it is not
(though its echoes enclose me   )

shifting on a surface   among many
                the mind   going into

Shape-shifters (1)

Incomers on a grandiose street corner
wonder tilts our faces
                         to a sheer fall
                         of sheeting water

It might be self-cleaning glass
or an urban waterfall
in the form of a cursive script

a formation of steel and air   transformed
in the sky's reflection   transforms

images
of what a window might show us
                         as if made of flickerings
                         our lives
in this city's
                         shades of shifting weather

Frequencies of Visible Light
(Loch Lomond to the Clyde: the River Leven)

By Moss o' Balloch   the iris of the eye
takes in frequencies of visible light
(three bridges a river begins and ends with)

is taken in by the invisible   (the particles
of luminous dials   targets of living tissue)
not yet decontaminated

Below cylinders of barrage
a lattice of footbridge   (deconstructed
          in our common mouths
          from ownership to speckled mimic)

The talking   broad as the flow of water
and wire and wall   (iron-braced
          to cage a red so fast and brilliant
          it would not fade in water or sunlight)
          the fumes and knowledge of a secretive regime
          a colour that subsumed all others

From chemical bonds to whisky bonds
a trace absorbed by the spirit
a distillate evaporates into air
          the angels' share

          is brought to light
in soot-black fungus   encrusted
branches of buddleia   silhouetted
against the spectrum of visible light

The river in its always present moment
pooling to a point smaller than a tarnished coin
          (a bawbee for the Bawbee Brig)
          a rainbow over a vale of tears

A fisherman in a froth of sun and shadow
(mottled belly of sea trout   spring salmon
shoaling in the hidden pools)   unspools

    a kaleidoscope
    of parrots and strutting peacocks
    yellow-flowered chromate of lead
celandine and wood anemones

A metallic span   (enough to drop a body down
not fishing but fished from water)
rises up to a lattice of light

    as if a boy bolted together Meccano, a kit
    fixed at the odd angles of its era

    the tick-tock of the morning shift
    crossing the river to make time
    for General Time   (not yet digital)
    a clock for every home

    A sight for sore eyes   the play
    of sun on water   reflected waves
    in their shades   in the glare of summer
    eyes only for light   vertically polarized

    In the air good vibrations

    and a Polaroid snap
    of the latest glossy moment
    the oh so instant
    up-to-the-minute image

    not yet tipping towards the digital
    made a version of the present

gone the way the bleachfields went (soured in the sun's glare)
Construction Site Keep Out: this ground / that space in air
sold for development or

      sold down the river   gone south
      or east with the patterned saris, bolts
      of gorgeous cloth

or simply gone   a glint of pebbles
ploughing into the wide lower reaches of the A82
a marsh of pylons and willow scrub

      In a blue haze of scattering light
      a sick king   hunting for his own heart
      startles from conjured grasses
      a bird of paradise

the white-yellow wings of the butterflies
the white-grey wings of the heron

It begins and ends with bridges   riff of water
under arched stone   igneous closure

time   (no longer General)
slipping us downriver   towards the virtual
      shimmer of tides
      the salmon will pour their silver streaming into

Shape-shifters (2)

Visitors to an elegant, peopled square
faces tilted to swifts in flight
                              shrill, deft

describers of dark arabesques
above the perfect renaissance
                              plan of light

wordless   we watch them
                  chase high summer insects
in thunderstorm air   in flight
                              too fast for sight

as if they could tell us
                              what unknowable

ungrounded
                  shape-shifters in another air

Locksmith

What can I tell you
walking over walls and fences

turning aside out of the wind's strike
into a deep spit of forest dark
a trick of sun and shelter

at the left hand   a gate
locked fast by snow
rime smashed by wind through gaps of wire

a bare framework
of bones   of beasts and gate

of what is hidden   unpicked by light

deer talk
(in Little Druim Wood)

shout-louts
clod-footing through mud
odd body bright things
not ear-lifting
to wind   body   tree
squash underfoot
bark crisp tasty gills

watch   little body
the wind
does not enter
with nose talk
hoof tapping
you are   ear up
and shifting
wait

lift nose slow
only their light and dark
their out-of-place
not going between the trees
only in clear space
the hind-hoofers
strange ones under birch roof
wait

ear snap
eye gone
odd bodies
take their spell away

fast   little body
into ferny place
soft under hooves

through leaf net
into tree shade
frond flitter
ear-lift to leaf shift
nose to body reek
hidden
in sweet nodding cud
under stipple grass

in myriad

A Measure
(on Creag Mac Rànaich)

In bright cold we notch up
a rusted tally   the wire's lost measure
over knolled and shoaling snow

The only players here
ravens coasting on the wind's
       boundaryless transparence

and bolting, distant deer
their lace of hooves cut sharp as tin

Our tracks are pinned
on water frozen in the shape of a wave
diviners' rods cast to the wind

       a compass   invisible
except as a quill of bird or snow

       The weather's inkling
       vitrified to blades of ice
       shivers with a ring
       higher and lighter than glass

The lopsided fence posts magnify
in gaps and angles   the odd

human certainties
that set them there   resonant

Sinusoid
(on Cruach Ardrain)

glint of snow
    of mica in the schist
sinuous path replicates
quartz rills, silver
    on grey height

    echoes (harmonic)
steep earth's pitched gradient
cracked after winter
pitched sinister above a deep coire

frost heave
    splintering crazy paving
as fissures quartz might have oozed into
solidified to crust

the snow in flux (the twist of it)
on a path makes   (is made of)
a convoluted conduit
    under a twisting ridge

in swirling vapour
a replication   not exactitude
a folding over   a visual echo
    in the invisible
    waves of white light

elegy for a wild card
(under Creag Leacach)

crushed hare
flattened   comic hare
battened under snow
trodden under   hare as tread
                  hare as pattern
                  shattered skull
                  a jigsaw puzzle
                  of bones

skeletal
but best-dressed
in long furred mitts of paws
in mashed grey soil
colour of hare

knee joint
out of frame in bas-relief
the working hinge
of your dismantled
            lang shanks
            your named
            bones

            unbundled
            out of joint
            you're disassembled
            a flat-pack cartoonist
            wild card
            unbounded

In late October
(the Monadh Liath)

simply to be in this place
in the roar and the blue gold rush of it

the rusted fence, fallen wall
intense green of moss and bilberry

clocks half-turned   sun pitched in the sky
not low yet blinding

unable to measure arc or distance
to calculate what it means

what I know
is approximate   a rough thing, a vestige

hare and ptarmigan half-turned, white-bellied
                    not yet winter

just a moving forward into the wind
into the blue circumference
carrying with us the dead and the living

                    there is still time

fragments
half-formed, forming   shiver of vision

The complete and Wonderful Thing
for Fi

On the radio   a fragment   from another time zone
a numeral on the Richter scale   a cacophony of
                                         silence

jams landlines   all morning
multiplies in the ethernet's cloudy gaps
in empty inboxes   in the blank cells of phones
on the screen   across which a woman runs
                                         in fast shutter/flying forward
                                         beyond herself/
                                         beyond the city collapsing
                                         in the hubbub of lunchtime

or sleep's slow motion   nightmare of almost
                                         and who is lost behind her
                                         and where are our loved ones?

What was solid dissolves across a groundless field
                                         a woman struggling
                                         to reach her child

                           Hours later
              the signal between us   jagged
                  each *aftershock*   a gap between syllables
                     two just while I've been talking

                              her voice
          reassembles itself   out of the dark
                    across space
              complete and wonderful
into my afternoon's still ordinary light

The Life of the Field
for Lizzie

The place where you step over
the place where your daughter holds you
    I half imagine: the field
with its creek, the big trees, some of them fallen
a branch our daughters once sprung on together

Beyond the house a distant train
crosses the rough horizon of a ground
I can't, as you can, bring to mind in its detail
    grasses   tree bark   leaf mould
the clean stench of mud at the burn

        only the field   the idea of the field
        like a green skin   earth tissue
        and you finding your way through it
        in long grass   finding yourself

at the place where you used to jump
where now your foot won't work
Your body needled with information
won't assay the knowledge of landing
Your daughter finds you a stick, gives you her hand

        you step over   into the life of the field

Salmon Nets and the Sea
(after Joan Eardley)

A trailer, tipped up   identifier
by nets stretched to black frames, lit vermilion
a yellow flicker   out of browns wheeling into gunmetal
as gulls might do   inhabiting a band of foam and grit
    a hurled transforming density of being

The nets are lines flying across the field of vision
    into the creamy spill and drip of ocean
    sucked back to a blue deeper than translucence
petrol   and the sky oily dark
      (and the wheeling invisible gulls)

    yet nothing of steel
in the lowering spray, the flung moisture I stand in
cut by particles of the minute   invisible and indivisible
self dispersed   and coalescing
a bodily coherence   in the grit and oil of matter

Scree Music
(the Cuillin to Strath)

High on Garbh-bheinn
we cross from granite to gabbro
red to black

overlook   as a raven might
an aerial map   ragged fringe
of breach and breccia
a transitory battle ground
(fugitive between legend and history)

a gabbro wall built   (as if by giants)
by men bought cheaply to heave boulders through cloud
to divide the lord's forest from the Lord's summits
an old boundary that turns to granite
as the summits turn

where we fall away
like a speck in the eye of a bird

> the fringe of ravens' wings
> turning paired acrobatics
> over boundaries of rock
> and territory and weather

The ridge
a fire of black mineral
inaccessible water
a measurement of thirst

skin sweats salt over airy traverses
my own nervous fingering
unhabituated clumsy footwork
over invisibly distant detail
of crab shells and wrack
high tide mark   a visual echo

of the crater's broken circle
serrations of stacked gabbro   gullies   pinnacles
a tumble of blocks and shatterings
that which makes
scree music

a coire
    and what it contains
    snow
    or the ghost of snow
    ice
    or the ghost of ice
    roches moutonnées
    glacial striations
    look what the ice dragged in

the whole island
    done over with boulders

                    refrain   too soft a word
                    for what the cuckoo sings/or is
                    disturbing thief of nature
                    stealing the nurture of pipits' nests

The whole island
    done over with boulders

       .

        .

         .

            clearance cairns
      fields gone to rough ground

runrig
    as if natural
    long mounds patterning earth

the broken houses
    stacked gables
    gullied   crossed over

a bridge a single slab
my husband walks across (foot worn
         repeats the passage of generations
         but end-stopped)

a history of harshness and poverty
beauty and then the loss of it

like a funeral coronach
the long plaintive wail the geologist heard
(witness to rock and human lives)

                a skylark's rising
                flutter of song
                the pure note of our attention
                over fields gone to rough ground

Between Suisnish and Boreraig
islands afloat in haar   curved over the sgùrr
          laps in, almost over us

the shepherd's house   a rusting lacework
gone in its turn   beside that which it supplanted
the burned township

and we in our turn
walking onward   held in our present

          midges lifting to life
          not yet in clouds yet omnipresent
          heather buds forming
          or embryonic grass seed
          skin prickled
          cumulus budding – a fluorescence

early purple orchid   flower of the limestone
Strath Suardal a green sward because of it
a place of bounty and toil
because of a boundary
because of a transformation
how marble cut the limestone and was cut from limestone
its crystals polished to astonish
fine as Carrara, ornament to marvel over

the long-abandoned long wall
of the marble factory
beside the grave slabs of Cill Chriosd

          oystercatchers
          piping from the loch
          as if from a high tide mark
          of crab shells and wrack

Found 7th September 1940
a sailor of the merchant navy
known unto God

grounded here between
Mackinnon   Maclellan   Macintosh of Torrin

Second Engineer   Chief Engineer
Steam Trawler "William Humphries"

MacInnes who died at Boreraig   his wife, Catherine

William Matheson
the second year of the Great War

John McPherson in memory of Christy McKinnon
his beloved spouse

each memory
each letter erased
until the name is a reef inverted
a vanishing
as a floundering body gasps
grasps nothing   water or earth

and the passer-by reads only the surface

hoodie crows
on the green sward
sharp-eyed
glitter of bird mind

The walker on the track of the narrow-gauge
(past quarrymen   calcite dust in their lungs)

hears the stony rattle of the bogeys
altered in the kiln's hot core
to a mulch the colour of bone
to be shipped out
to make lush   other fields

to be shipped out
as people were shipped

        and of his wife
        and of his dearly beloved

to make a home anywhere
who learned how to make
and remake   the ordinary common life

              over them the swallow
              hi-tailing it
              feeding on air
              sings on a wire above gravel

and the passer-by   (not of this place)
observes the caravan out back
the tussocky scatter of sheep
the run on aftersun   the price of petrol
the everyday life which continues

the names which continue
on an island ringed by campervans
(slow-burning fuel of a seasonal migration)
at the verges   creeping buttercup
wrapped bouquets

the old narrow-windowed dwellings
side by side with new houses of sustainable larch
a gold that will turn grey   ageing in air

behind the holiday house
horses in the field

                              and over us
                              sounding together
                              birds of garden and woodland
                              thrush and blackbird

                              the delectable song

of our common life

Notes and Acknowledgements

'Transitional' was written as a part of a walking project, *The Bedrock Journey*, organised by the Royal Scottish Geographical Society and Speygrian Educational Trust, in which a group of artists and writers, along with a geologist and geographer, followed the old 'Thieves' Road' across Badenoch and Lochaber from Dalwhinnie through Corrour (where I joined them) to Glen Nevis. A draft of the poem was included in a Walking Library Book made by Dee Hedden and in the exhibition 'Once Upon a Journey' at the Scottish Storytelling Centre in 2013. A later version was published in *The Long Poem Magazine*.

'Seeded' was written in response to a visit to Dawyck Botanic Gardens during Gerry Loose's residency there as part of the *Walking with Poets* project (September 2013) and was originally published in Gerry's blog.

'Watershed': an east-west crossing of Scotland, with many thanks to Jean Langhorne for her company.

'Fire-working': a walk on the northern hills of the Rhinns of Kells surrounding the old Woodhead leadmine and township in Carsphairn, Galloway. A number of sources were particularly useful: the report by Joseph Fletcher into conditions at the neighbouring Leadhills mine (*The Children's Employment Commission 1842. On the employment of children and young persons in the lead-mines of the counties of Lanark and Dumfries; and on the state, condition, and treatment of such children and young persons*); an archaeological report by Cressey, M., Pickin, J., & Hicks, K., 2004. 'The Silver Rig, Pibble and Woodhead metal mines, Galloway, Scotland', *Mining Hist*, 15, 6, pp. 49-62; the 1851 Census Returns for the parish of Carsphairn, County of Kirkcudbrightshire (Carsphairn Heritage Centre) – poignant for the number of widows. www.scottishmining.co.uk is an excellent general resource on the history of mining in Scotland. Background on the covenanter John Dempster and whether he appears in the historical record can be found in *Jardine's Book of Martyrs* – http:drmarkjardine.wordpress.com

'Between Geology and Air' and 'Rope Piece' were written in response to exhibitions shown at the Fruitmarket Gallery, Edinburgh, in 2011.

'Frequencies of Visible Light' follows the course of the River Leven from Balloch to Dumbarton and was my contribution to *A Festschrift for Tony Frazer* http://tonyfrazer.weebly.com/. Tony spent some of his teenage years travelling from his home in Balloch to school in Dumbarton. *from ownership to speckled mimic* refers to the Stuckie Bridge: a corruption of Stirling Bridge to starling, known locally as a stuckie. See Gordon Burns' *Bridging the Leven*, Anderson, 2009.

In 'Sinusoid' and 'Scree Music' *coire* is written in the Gaelic of the place names (Coire Ardrain, Coire Lagan) rather than in its Scots form – *corrie*.

'The Life of the Field' was written for Elizabeth Burns.

'Salmon Nets and the Sea' was one of a number of commissioned poems written in response to Scottish paintings in the Hunterian Gallery, Glasgow, and published in *The Hunterian Poems*, edited by Alan Riach, Freight Books, 2015.

The ground of 'Scree Music' is southern Skye: the hills of Garbh-bheinn and Belig, Sgùrr MhicChoinnich on the Cuillin ridge, the cleared coastal townships of Suisnish and Boreraig, the marble quarries and burial ground of Cill Chriosd in Strath Suardal and the village of Harrapool.

Acknowledgements are due to the editors of *Blackbox Manifold*, *Long Poem Magazine*, *Molly Bloom*, *Northwords Now*, *Painted Spoken*, *Shearsman* and *X* (Red Squirrel Press and the Scottish Writers' Centre) where some of these poems originally appeared; also to St Mungo's Mirrorball and Glasgow Life who funded the Clydebuilt Verse Apprenticeships for which I was the mentor in 2013-14. In memory of and with thanks to Tom Leonard, with whom I'll continue to debate the unstable we. My thanks to Gerry Loose and Robyn Marsack who also read and commented on the collection; in addition, to Alan Riach, John Purser and all at Mashiters.

Deepest thanks go to my husband, Tom Prentice, with whom I have shared most of these landscapes, and whose knowledge and detailed observation of the Scottish hills underlie so many of the poems.